NFTS Unlocked!

A Creator's Guide to Understanding and Profiting
from Non-Fungible Tokens

Dr. Asuquo Hogan-Bassey

DEDICATION

First of all, to God, the Ultimate Creator of all things who gives us the privilege to create in his image, and also with lots of love to my amazing children, Deborah, Emmanuel and David who never stopped believing in me especially when I needed it most, even when believing did not seem to make much sense.

CONTENTS

ACKNOWLEDGMENTS

I acknowledge my amazing family and your patience with me on the quest to make this book a possibility. I also acknowledge all the greats that have done foundational work making this research possible. This is truly a case of seeing farther because I have had the privilege of standing on the shoulder of giants. I also acknowledge every creative saddled with the responsibility of adding value to this world through the visions that enter their hearts. Your burden is instrumental to the drive that created this work..

1 INTRODUCTION TO NON FUNGIBLE TOKENS

NFTs, or non-fungible tokens, are a type of digital asset that use block-chain technology to certify their ownership and authenticity.

They have become popular in recent years as a way for creators to monetize their digital creations, from artwork and music to virtual real estate and even tweets.

A wide range of opportunities and possibilities exist with NFTs. The trend first caught my attention when I heard a particular creator of very innovative tech enabled artistic furniture mention that he had created NFTs around some of his novel creations. As at then, one of the creations was valued at about 400,000 USD.

My interest increased when I heard my digital marketing mentor, Russell Brunson mention he was collecting some very rare old books and creating NFTs around them that would enable the general public buy into ownership of these rare and valuable works similar in my understanding to shares. This got me interested and informed this research into NFTs.

This book is intended as the creator's guide into the fascinating world of Non Fungible Tokens.

For a while, I was drawn to the topic and had a few ideas to deploy, but needed guidance. My hunger around the topic led me to research content and experts resulting in this book.

If you are a creator with intellectual property of value, NFTs are definitely something to explore,

In this book, we will consider the process of creating and selling NFTs, from conceptualization to marketing.

NFTs, or non-fungible tokens, are unique digital assets that are verified on a blockchain network. Most of the time the Etherum Blockchain is preferred for NFT verification due to the smart contract feature of this network.

Unlike cryptocurrencies such as Bitcoin, which are fungible and interchangeable, each NFT is one-of-a-kind and cannot be replicated or exchanged for another NFT.

NFTs can represent a wide range of digital content, including artwork, music, videos, virtual real estate, and even tweets. They are often used in the art world as a way for artists to monetize their digital creations. Physical assets can also be converted to NFTs, such as the examples of the books and novel furniture that I mentioned earlier on. I personally believe the possibilities are enormous with a little out of the box thinking.

 Non fungible tokens are often used in the art world as a way for artists to monetize their digital creations as they can be bought and sold on online marketplaces for cryptocurrency.

The ownership and authenticity of NFTs are verified using blockchain technology, which ensures that the ownership of an NFT is transparent and immutable. This means once created, the information concerning its ownership becomes public information on the ledger and this cannot be changed in the manner of blockchain smart contracts.

 Because of their uniqueness and the ability to verify ownership, NFTs have become a popular way for creators to monetize their creativity.

It has also created novel opportunity for collectors and investors to invest in and collect digital assets.

2 CHOOSING YOUR NFT CONCEPT

The first step in creating an NFT is to come up with a concept. It could be an original artwork, a digital collectible, a piece of music, or even a tweet. The key is to create something that is unique and appealing to potential buyers. It's also important to package value in your NFT offer. When the NFT craze started, many people jumped on the bandwagon with the erroneous belief that people would value and purchase an NFT just because it was an NFT. The rules of the marketplace are timeless; people will only purchase what they consider truly useful and valuable.

In this chapter, we will discuss how to choose your NFT concept and how to ensure that it is valuable to buyers.

Non-Fungible Tokens (NFTs) have taken the world by storm, with billions of dollars in transactions made in the past few years. However, not all NFTs are created equal, and not all of them have the same value. The key to creating a successful NFT is to choose a viable and valuable concept. In this chapter, we will guide you through the process of choosing a viable NFT concept that has the potential to be successful.

Demystifying NFTs

Before we dive into the process of choosing a viable NFT concept, it is important to once again remember what NFTs are and how they work.

NFTs are unique digital assets that are stored on a blockchain.

Each NFT is one-of-a-kind and cannot be replicated or duplicated. NFTs can be anything from art, music, videos, to virtual real estate, gaming assets, and more.

They are typically bought and sold using crypto-currency, with transactions recorded on a blockchain.

You can think of an NFT as a unique cryptographic token created to represent creative works, digital assets and the like.

The cryptographic tokens are stored on a blockchain network.

This means to create an NFT, you first of all create or identify an asset, exclusively own it, then convert it into a non-fungible token (or more appropriately, represent it with a cryptographic token) through a minting process.

We will x ray the process of selecting the right asset to convert to an NFT. It is of course reasonable to connect what kind of asset or concept you will utilize for an NFT with the audience it is created for.

Identify Your Target Audience

The first step in choosing a viable NFT concept is to identify your target audience.

Who are you creating the NFT for?

What are their interests, hobbies, and passions?

What are their fears? What are their pain points? What are the deep dreams and desires they would love to achieve?

Who are their heroes and role models?

Who are they exactly? And where do they hang out online?

Create an avatar for your target audience. This will help put you in their thinking frame and thus help your creative process. Knowing where they hang out will also help your marketing outreach when your NFT is created.

Understanding your target audience will help you create an NFT that resonates with them and has the potential to be valuable. For example, if your target audience is music lovers, you may consider creating an NFT that features exclusive access to a concert or backstage passes.

Research Existing NFTs

Once you have identified your target audience, it is important to research existing NFTs. This will help you identify gaps in the market and ensure that your NFT concept is unique and valuable. Look at the top-selling NFTs and try to understand what makes them successful. This will give you an idea of what works and what doesn't.

Brainstorm NFT Concepts

Now that you have an understanding of your target audience and the market, it is time to brainstorm NFT concepts. Start with a broad concept and then refine it. Consider what makes your NFT unique, how it will be used, and what value it will bring to the buyer. You may consider consulting with experts in the field or hiring a professional to help you refine your concept.

Validate Your NFT Concept

Once you have a refined NFT concept, it is time to validate it. This means testing it with your target audience to ensure that it resonates with them. You may consider creating a survey, hosting a focus group, or conducting interviews with potential buyers. This will help you identify any issues with your concept and make adjustments before launching it.

Launch and Market Your NFT

Finally, it is time to launch and market your NFT. This involves creating a compelling listing that highlights the unique features and benefits of your NFT. At this point it is important to have created a compelling valuable offer for your audience. Clearly highlight the value of your NFT with an attractive stack. A stack is a listing that clearly shows everything included in your NFT offer as well as the value of that particular feature. Remember that value and cost is not the same thing. A simple way to think of value is what it actually is worth. While the cost is how much you sell you package.

Employ what I love to call the 10x value rule. This means, if you intend to sell a package for $1000, you should be able to bundle enough value that would sensibly go for $10,000.

You will also need to market your NFT to your target audience through social media, email marketing joint ventures, affiliates and other available channels. A major mistake most creators make when it comes to their NFTs is the assumption that their creations will get found and purchased by their target audience simply by listing it on a marketplace. There will be need to actively market your created NFT through available marketing and distribution channels just like you would have to market any digital creation or physical product.

Be sure to track your results and adjust your marketing strategy as needed.

Choosing a viable NFT concept is the key to creating a successful NFT. By understanding your target audience, researching the market, brainstorming concepts, and validating your ideas, you can create an NFT that resonates with buyers and has the potential to be valuable. Remember to focus on creating something unique and valuable, and to always test and adjust your ideas based on feedback.

3 THE BLOCKCHAIN AND YOUR NON FUNGIBLE TOKEN

Once you have your concept, the next step is to create your NFT but before we delve into the technicalities of creating and minting your NFT, It's important to understand the blockchain, the underlying technology that allows NFTs to run.

A digital asset is minted as an NFT and has to be hosted on a blockchain platform.

It is thus important to understand the importance of the blockchain as it pertains to NFTs and data storage.

Creating an NFT will fundamentally involve creating or identifying an asset, securing its ownership and minting it as an NFT on a blockchain platform. The asset could actually be digital, or physical. The important thing is that it is represented as a cryptographic token and stored on the blockchain as an NFT.

In this chapter, we will explore the technical aspects of creating an NFT, including choosing a blockchain platform, creating your digital asset, and minting your NFT.

Non-fungible tokens (NFTs) have become a popular way to represent assets on the blockchain. NFTs provide a way to represent unique, indivisible, and rare assets like art, music, video, and other digital assets. In this book, we will explore the process of creating and minting your NFT.

Understanding the Blockchain

The blockchain is the technology that underpins NFTs. In this chapter, we will explore how the blockchain works, what it is, and how it differs from traditional centralized systems. We will also explore the different blockchain platforms and which ones are best suited for NFT creation.

The Blockchain is a digital ledger that allows multiple parties to record and track transactions in a secure and transparent manner. It is a decentralized, distributed database that stores information in the form of blocks, which are linked together in a chronological and immutable chain.

Each block contains a unique cryptographic code, called a hash, which is created by combining the data stored in the block with the hash of the previous block in the chain. This creates a permanent and tamper-proof record of each transaction, which can be verified and validated by all participants in the network.

Blockchains are often associated with cryptocurrencies like Bitcoin, but they have many other potential applications, such as supply chain management, digital identity verification, and smart contracts.

Their relevance in digital identity verification and smart contracts make them very useful for managing the concept of NFTs which in most cases involves a digital form of intellectual property ownership verification management for physical or digital assets and art.

 Because they are decentralized, blockchains offer a high degree of security and transparency, making them a popular choice for a wide range of industries and use cases.

How the Blockchain Works

In this section, we will delve deeper into the technical details of blockchain technology. We will explain the basics of hashing, public and private keys, and digital signatures, all of which are fundamental components of blockchain technology. We will also explore the different types of blockchain, including public, private, and hybrid, and how they are used in various applications and especially with relevance to NFTs. At this point, I want to acknowledge the fact that not all creators are tech inclined and some of this information may initially seem a bit overwhelming, but we will do our best to simplify the information as much as possible. It is also important to note that to harness the power of nfts to monetize your creations, it is not compulsory to become a n authority on the blockchain, but a basic knowledge of the concepts of blockchain technology will definitely be helpful.

The Blockchain is a distributed database that allows a network of computers to maintain a continuously growing list of records, called blocks, which are linked and secured using cryptography.

The basic principles of how the blockchain works are as follows:

Decentralization:

The blockchain network is decentralized, meaning that it is not controlled by a single entity or authority. Instead, it is a distributed network of computers or nodes that work together to maintain the blockchain ledger.

Blocks: The blockchain is made up of blocks, which are bundles of data that are cryptographically secured and linked together in chronological order to form a chain. Each block contains a unique code, called a hash, which identifies it and links it to the previous block in the chain.

Verification:

 To add a new block to the chain, the network of computers must first verify and confirm the transactions in the block. This verification process is done through a consensus mechanism, where a majority of the network nodes must agree that the block is valid before it is added to the chain.

Security:

The blockchain is secured using advanced cryptographic techniques, including public-key cryptography and digital signatures, to ensure that the data in the blocks cannot be tampered with or altered.

Transparency:

The blockchain ledger is publicly accessible and transparent, meaning that anyone can view the transactions on the network, though some blockchains can offer privacy features.

Immutability:

Once a block is added to the blockchain, it is almost impossible to alter or delete the data contained within it. This makes the blockchain a highly reliable and trustworthy database for storing and verifying digital information

Overall, the blockchain is a secure, decentralized, and transparent way to record and verify digital transactions, making it a powerful tool for a variety of applications, such as cryptocurrency, supply chain management, digital identity and smart contracts with relevance to NFTs

Cryptocurrencies, Digital Assets and Blockchain

Now we will focus on the relationship between cryptocurrencies, digital assets and blockchain. We will explain what digital assets and cryptocurrencies are, how they are created, and how they can be used.

Digital assets, cryptocurrencies, and blockchain technology are all closely related concepts that have gained significant attention in recent years.

A digital asset is any form of information or data that has value and can be owned or controlled by a person or organization. Digital assets can be in various forms, including digital art, music, videos, online courses, and more. When an NFT is created, you can think of it as digitalizing an asset in such a manner as to have its records on the blockchain and assigning a unique token to it. Some NFTs could be physical assets. In most cases, minting them as NFTs could also involve creating a digital version or representation that will in turn be represented as a cryptographic token or NFT.

Cryptocurrencies, on the other hand, are a type of digital asset that utilizes cryptography to secure transactions and control the creation of new units. They are typically decentralized and operate on a peer-to-peer network, which means they are not controlled by any central authority or government.

The blockchain is the underlying technology that enables cryptocurrencies and NFTs to function. It is a distributed ledger technology that records transactions in a secure and transparent manner. Every transaction on a blockchain is recorded on a block, and each block is linked to the previous one, forming a chain of blocks.

Blockchain technology has various benefits, including transparency, security, and decentralization. It eliminates the need for intermediaries, which reduces the cost of transactions and increases efficiency.

Overall, digital assets, cryptocurrencies, and blockchain technology have the potential to revolutionize various industries and change the way we think about value exchange and ownership of assets.

4 NFT STANDARDS, SMART CONTRACTS AND MINTING NFTS

Once you have your concept, the next step is to create your NFT.

This involves creating a digital asset and minting it as an NFT on a blockchain platform.

In this chapter, we will explore the different NFT standards, including ERC-721 and ERC-1155. We will also explore their differences.

 We will delve into smart contracts, which are self-executing contracts allowing for the creation and transfer of NFTs.

NFT Standards

One of the first things to understand when creating an NFT is the various NFT standards that exist. There are two main NFT standards used in the industry, ERC-721 and ERC-1155, both of which are based on the Ethereum blockchain.

ERC-721

This is the most common NFT standard and is used to create unique, one-of-a-kind NFTs. This standard is ideal for artists and creators who want to sell digital art, music, or other unique content. Each ERC-721 token is unique and has its own set of properties, making them highly valuable to collectors.

ERC-1155

This is a newer NFT standard that allows for the creation of both unique and fungible tokens. This standard is ideal for gaming and other applications where multiple copies of an NFT are needed. With ERC-1155, creators can create multiple copies of the same NFT, making it easier to distribute their content to a larger audience.

Smart Contracts

Smart contracts are an essential part of the NFT ecosystem. Smart contracts are self-executing contracts that are stored on the blockchain and automatically execute when certain conditions are met. In the case of NFTs, smart contracts are used to create, buy, and sell NFTs without the need for intermediaries.

Smart contracts are written in a programming language called Solidity, which is specifically designed for use on the Ethereum blockchain. When creating a smart contract, you will need to define the conditions under which the contract will execute. For example, you might create a smart contract that automatically transfers ownership of an NFT to a buyer once they have paid the seller.

Gas Prices

Gas prices are another essential aspect of the NFT ecosystem. Gas is the fee that is paid to the Ethereum network for processing a transaction. Gas prices are measured in Gwei, and the price can fluctuate depending on network activity.

When creating and transferring NFTs, it's important to choose the right gas price to ensure that your transaction is processed quickly and efficiently. If you set the gas price too low, your transaction may take a long time to process, or it may fail altogether. If you set the gas price too high, you may end up paying more than you need to.

Wallets

Wallets are the final piece of the NFT puzzle. A wallet is a software program that allows you to store your NFTs and interact with the Ethereum blockchain. There are several different types of wallets available, including hardware wallets, desktop wallets, and mobile wallets.

When choosing a wallet, it's important to consider security, ease of use, and compatibility with the Ethereum blockchain. Hardware wallets are considered the most secure option, as they store your private keys offline. Desktop and mobile wallets are more convenient but may be less secure.

Creating Your NFT,

We will now discuss the steps involved in creating your NFT, including designing your artwork, choosing the right blockchain platform, and creating your smart contract. We will also explore different tools and platforms that can be used to create your NFT, including OpenSea, Rarible, and Mintable.

Creating an NFT (Non-Fungible Token) involves creating a unique digital asset and assigning it to a blockchain. Here are the general steps to create and load an NFT to the blockchain:

Choose the blockchain:

Select the blockchain platform you want to use. Ethereum is the most popular platform for NFTs, but other platforms like Binance Smart Chain, Flow, and Polygon are gaining popularity.

Choose an NFT standard:

Decide which NFT standard you want to use. ERC-721 and ERC-1155 are the most commonly used standards on Ethereum. Each standard has its own set of rules for creating and managing NFTs.

Create your digital asset:

Create a unique digital asset that you want to tokenize as an NFT. This asset could be anything from a digital artwork to a virtual real estate property. You can also create NFTs that are linked to physical assets such as old rare books, or physical artwork. There will be a lot of relevance for this in the future as it will create the possibility of a great number of people being able to buy into ownership of extremely expensive and valuable work they would not have been able to own alone.

Mint the NFT:

To mint an NFT, you need to use a smart contract on the blockchain platform. The smart contract will handle the creation and management of your NFT. You can use a platform like OpenSea, Mintable, or Rarible to mint your NFT.

Load the NFT:

After you have minted the NFT, you need to load it onto the blockchain. This involves paying a gas fee to the blockchain network to verify the transaction and add it to the blockchain.

Store the NFT:

Once your NFT is loaded onto the blockchain, it is stored in your digital wallet. You can use your wallet to manage and transfer your NFT as needed.

Note that creating and loading an NFT can be a complex process, especially if you are new to blockchain and smart contracts. It is important to do your research and follow best practices to ensure that your NFT is created and loaded correctly

Minting Your NFT

Minting your NFT involves the intricacies of uploading your digital asset to the blockchain and creating a unique token that represents it. In this section, we will attempt to simplify the steps involved in minting your NFT, including choosing the right gas price, setting up your wallet, and executing your smart contract.

Minting an NFT is the process of creating a unique digital asset and adding it to the blockchain. In this section, we will go through the steps involved in minting your own NFT, from choosing your NFT standards to uploading your content to a marketplace.

Step 1: Choose Your NFT Standard

The first step in minting your NFT is to choose your NFT standard. As mentioned earlier, there are two main NFT standards used in the industry, ERC-721 and ERC-1155. Depending on your use case, you may choose to use one or both of these standards.

Step 2: Create Your Smart Contract

Once you have chosen your NFT standard, you will need to create a smart contract. Smart contracts are written in Solidity, a programming language used on the Ethereum blockchain. If you are not familiar with Solidity, there are several online resources that can help you get started.

In your smart contract, you will define the properties of your NFT, such as its name, symbol, and any additional metadata you want to include. You will also need to define the conditions under which your NFT can be bought, sold, or transferred.

Step 3: Mint Your NFT

With your smart contract in place, you can now mint your NFT. To do this, you will need to use a tool like Remix or Truffle to compile and deploy your smart contract to the Ethereum blockchain.

Once your smart contract is deployed, you can use a tool like OpenSea or Mintable to mint your NFT. These platforms allow you to upload your content, such as a digital image or music file, and attach it to your NFT.

Step 4: Set Your NFT Price

Once your NFT is minted, you will need to set a price for it. You can choose to sell your NFT for a fixed price or put it up for auction.

If you choose to sell your NFT for a fixed price, you can set the price in your smart contract. If you choose to put your NFT up for auction, you can use a platform like OpenSea to create an auction and set the starting bid and duration.

Step 5: Transfer Your NFT

Once your NFT is sold, the final step is to transfer it to the buyer. This is done through the Ethereum blockchain, and the transfer will be recorded on the blockchain for transparency and immutability.

To transfer your NFT, you will need to use a wallet that supports the ERC-721 or ERC-1155 standards, such as MetaMask or MyEtherWallet. You will also need to know the buyer's wallet address and initiate the transfer through the platform where the sale took place.

Minting an NFT may seem complicated at first, but with the right tools and resources, anyone can do it. By following these steps and taking the time to understand the NFT ecosystem, you can create and sell your own unique digital content as an NFT

.

5. MARKETING AND SELLING YOUR NON FUNGIBLE TOKEN

There are a number of ways to market and sell NFTs and we will explore a few of them, we will also x-ray important considerations to set you up for success in selling your NFTs , including setting the right price, creating a marketing campaign, and using social media to promote your NFT. We will also discuss the different marketplaces that can be used to sell your NFT, including OpenSea, SuperRare, and Nifty Gateway.

To sell your NFT, you need to create a marketing strategy that will attract potential buyers. We will explore different marketing strategies, including social media marketing, influencer marketing, and auction sites. We will also discuss how to create a strong brand identity and build a following for your NFT.

One of the most challenging aspects of selling NFTs is determining the right price. In this chapter, we will discuss how to set a fair price for your NFT and how to determine its value based on factors like rarity, uniqueness, and market demand.

Finally, in this chapter, we will discuss how to sell your NFT. We will explore different platforms for selling NFTs, including OpenSea, Rarible, and SuperRare. We will also discuss the legal aspects of selling NFTs, including copyright and intellectual property rights.

Setting Your Price

One of the most important things to consider when selling an NFT is pricing. The right price can attract buyers and increase the likelihood of a sale, while an incorrect price can turn buyers away. When setting your price, consider the following factors:

Rarity: If your NFT is rare or one-of-a-kind, you can price it higher than a more common NFT.

Uniqueness: The more unique your NFT is, the more valuable it becomes.

Market demand: Consider the current demand for NFTs in your category or niche. If there is high demand, you can price your NFT higher.

It's important to research other NFTs in your category or niche to get an idea of the market value. You can also use online tools such as CryptoArtPulse or CryptoSlam to check the sales history and price of similar NFTs.

Creating a Marketing Campaign

Once you've determined your price, it's time to create a marketing campaign to promote your NFT. Here are some marketing strategies to consider:

Social Media Marketing:

Utilize social media platforms such as Twitter, Instagram, and TikTok to promote your NFT. You can create engaging posts, run paid ads, and collaborate with influencers to reach a wider audience.

Influencer Marketing:

 Partnering with an influencer in your niche who can help you reach their followers and increase your NFT's exposure. Reach out to influencers and offer them a commission for promoting your NFT to their followers.

Email Marketing:

Collect emails from potential buyers and use them to send newsletters, updates, and promotions. You can use email marketing platforms such as Mailchimp or

ConvertKit to create and send newsletters.

Building a Brand Identity

Having a strong brand identity can help you stand out in a crowded NFT marketplace. Here are some tips to consider when building your brand identity:

Consistent Branding: Use consistent branding across all your marketing channels, including your website, social media, and email marketing campaigns.

Unique Logo and Design: Invest in a unique logo and design that reflects your brand identity and values.

Brand Story: Create a compelling brand story that resonates with your audience and sets you apart from the competition

Selling Your NFT

There are many online marketplaces where you can sell your NFT, including:

OpenSea:

OpenSea is the largest NFT marketplace with a wide range of categories and price ranges. You can create and sell your NFT directly on the platform.

Rarible:

Rarible is a decentralized marketplace where you can mint and sell your NFT. You can also sell limited edition NFTs and use the platform's auction feature.

SuperRare:

SuperRare is a curated marketplace for high-quality NFTs. You need to apply to become a creator, and the platform takes a 15% commission on all sales.

When selling your NFT, make sure to provide clear descriptions, high-quality images, and accurate pricing. You can also consider offering limited editions or creating a series to increase the perceived value of your NFT. Finally, make sure to stay up-to-date with the latest NFT trends and market demands to stay competitive

.

6 STORING AND TRANSFERRING YOUR NON FUNGIBLE TOKEN

In this chapter, we will discuss the best practices for storing and transferring your NFT, including using cold storage, setting up multi-sig wallets, and transferring your NFT to different wallets and platforms. We will also explore the different use cases for NFTs, including gaming, art, music, and collectibles.

Storing Your NFTs

Storing your NFTs properly is crucial for ensuring their safety and security. One of the best ways to store your NFTs is by using a hardware wallet, such as Ledger or Trezor. These wallets are designed to keep your private keys offline and away from the internet, reducing the risk of hacking and theft. You can also use a software wallet, such as MetaMask, but it's important to make sure that your computer is free of malware and viruses to prevent any security breaches.

Another way to store your NFTs is by using cold storage. This involves storing your private keys offline, either on a USB drive or a paper wallet. Cold storage is a good option for those who want an added layer of security, but it can be cumbersome to use and may require more technical knowledge.

Setting up multi-sig wallets is also a popular way to store NFTs. A multi-sig wallet requires multiple parties to sign off on transactions, making it more secure and less susceptible to hacking. This is especially useful for high-value NFTs or for businesses that handle multiple NFTs.

Transferring Your NFTs

Transferring your NFTs involves sending them from one wallet to another. The process is similar to sending cryptocurrency, but it's important to make sure that you're sending the NFT to the correct address and that the receiving wallet is compatible with the NFT's blockchain.

Before transferring your NFT, make sure to double-check the receiving address and confirm that it's the correct one. Once you've confirmed the address, initiate the transfer from your wallet and wait for the confirmation on the blockchain.

If you need to transfer your NFT to a different platform or marketplace, such as from OpenSea to Rarible, you'll need to follow the platform's specific transfer process. This may involve creating a new account or wallet on the platform and then initiating the transfer from your original wallet.

Use Cases for NFTs

NFTs have a variety of use cases, including gaming, art, music, and collectibles. In the gaming industry, NFTs are used to represent in-game items and assets, such as weapons and characters. In the art world, NFTs are used to represent digital art pieces, providing a way for artists to sell and authenticate their work. In the music industry, NFTs are used to represent unique pieces of music or concert tickets, giving fans a new way to connect with their favorite artists. And in the collectibles industry, NFTs are used to represent rare and unique items, such as trading cards or historical artifacts.

Understanding how to store and transfer your NFTs is essential for maintaining their value and ensuring their safety. By following best practices and using secure wallets and platforms, you can feel confident in the security of your NFTs.

7 NON FUNGIBLE TOKENS AND THE FUTURE

In this chapter, we will explore the future of NFTs, including their potential to disrupt traditional industries and the impact they could have on the creative economy. We will also discuss the potential risks and challenges associated with NFTs, including scalability, interoperability, and regulation.

 NFTs have become a popular way to represent digital assets on the blockchain. In this book, we have explored the process of creating and minting your NFT, including the technical aspects involved in the process. I believe by now you have been provided with the knowledge and tools needed to create and market your own NFT.

The future of NFTs is a topic that excites many experts in the blockchain and creative spaces. There are already numerous ways in which NFTs are disrupting traditional industries and creating new opportunities for artists, musicians, and other creatives. One of the most significant advantages of NFTs is that they provide a secure and transparent way to verify ownership and authenticity of digital assets. This opens up new possibilities for the distribution of digital content and new forms of monetization.

One area where NFTs are already having a major impact is in the gaming industry. Game developers can use NFTs to create unique in-game items that players can own and trade on various marketplaces. This creates new revenue streams for game developers and also gives players a greater sense of ownership over their in-game assets. We're already seeing many innovative uses of NFTs in the gaming space, and this trend is likely to continue.

NFTs are also changing the way we think about art and other forms of creative expression. With NFTs, artists can create and sell unique digital artworks that are verifiably one-of-a-kind. This creates new opportunities for artists to monetize their work and bypass traditional gatekeepers in the art world. In addition, NFTs provide a new way for collectors to build and showcase their collections, as well as a new way for artists to connect with their fans and build a following.

Another area where NFTs are likely to make a big impact is in the music industry. Musicians can use NFTs to create unique digital albums or individual tracks that fans can own and trade. This creates new revenue streams for musicians and also provides a new way for fans to connect with their favorite artists.

However, as with any new technology, there are also potential risks and challenges associated with NFTs. One of the biggest challenges is scalability. As more people start using NFTs, the underlying blockchain technology may struggle to handle the increased demand. This could lead to slower transaction times and higher fees.

Interoperability is also a challenge. Currently, there are many different blockchain networks and marketplaces that support NFTs, but they are not always compatible with each other. This makes it difficult for buyers and sellers to move NFTs between different platforms.

Regulation is another potential challenge. As NFTs become more main-stream, it's likely that regulators will start paying closer attention to the space. This could lead to new regulations and compliance requirements that could be difficult for smaller marketplaces and artists to comply with.

Despite these challenges, the future of NFTs is bright. They offer new opportunities for creators and provide a more transparent and secure way to verify ownership and authenticity of digital assets. As the technology continues to evolve, we're likely to see even more innovative uses of NFTs emerge in the years to come

8 NON FUNGIBLE TOKEN CASE STUDIES

I decided to compile a few NFT creation case studies in this chapter to allow our minds explore the limitless possibilities for creators with just a little bit of imagination.

1. The First Tweet Ever Sold as an NFT"

In March 2021, Twitter CEO Jack Dorsey sold his first-ever tweet as an NFT for a staggering $2.9 million. The tweet, which read "just setting up my twttr," was posted in March 2006 and was purchased by Sina Estavi, CEO of the blockchain platform Bridge Oracle. The sale made headlines around the world, as it was one of the first instances of a social media post being sold as an NFT.

2. The Mona Lisa NFT

In June 2021, the Louvre Museum in Paris created an NFT version of the Mona Lisa, one of the world's most famous paintings. The NFT, which was created in collaboration with the blockchain platform Binance, features a high-resolution digital image of the painting, along with a digital certificate of authenticity. The NFT was sold at auction for over $60 million, making it one of the most expensive NFTs ever sold. The identity of the buyer remains unknown.

3. From Book to NFT: The Case of 'The Great Gatsby

In August 2021, a first edition of F. Scott Fitzgerald's classic novel "The Great Gatsby" was converted into an NFT and sold at auction for $150,000. The book, which was published in 1925, features the author's signature and several annotations. The NFT version of the book includes a digital copy of the original text, along with additional multimedia content, such as audio recordings and videos of the author's life. The buyer was a collector who wishes to remain anonymous.

4. The World's First NFT Sneakers

In March 2021, the digital fashion house RTFKT Studios created the world's first NFT sneakers, which were sold for $3.1 million. The sneakers, which exist only in the digital realm, were designed in collaboration with the musician Deadmau5 and feature intricate 3D designs and animations. The NFT sneakers were purchased by a cryptocurrency investor named "Metakovan," who has since made headlines for his other high-profile NFT purchases.

5. The CryptoPunk Auction

In June 2021, a collection of 101 CryptoPunk NFTs was sold at auction for over $69 million. CryptoPunks are a series of 10,000 unique digital characters, created by the software company Larva Labs in 2017. Each character is completely unique and can be bought and sold on blockchain marketplaces. The auction included some of the rarest CryptoPunks, including one that sold for over $11 million.

The buyers were a mix of crypto investors, celebrities, and art collectors, all vying for a piece of this new digital art market.

6. The First-Ever NFT Artwork-

"Everydays: The First 5000 Days" by digital artist Beeple sold for $69 million at Christie's in March 2021. The artwork is a digital collage of images created by the artist every day over a period of 13 years. The sale marked the first time a major auction house sold a purely digital artwork as an NFT.

7. NFT Digital Land –

Decentraland is a blockchain-based virtual world where users can buy, sell, and develop virtual real estate. In February 2021, a parcel of virtual land in the game sold for over $1 million, making it one of the most expensive NFT sales to date.

8. The NFT Music Album-

In March 2021, the DJ and music producer Blau sold an album as an NFT for $11.6 million. The album, titled "Ultraviolet," was sold as a collection of unique NFTs that included exclusive rights to unreleased music, merchandise, and VIP experiences.

9. NFTs for Good –

The digital artist Krista Kim sold an NFT artwork for $500,000, with proceeds going to charity in March 2021. The artwork, titled "Mars House," is a virtual rendering of a futuristic home designed by Kim.

10. The World's First NFT Car-

In May 2021, a one-of-a-kind McLaren Speedtail was sold as an NFT for $2.5 million. The car was sold as a digital rendering that included exclusive access to the physical car and a bespoke experience with McLaren.

11. The NFT Luxury Handbag –

In March 2021, a digital version of a limited-edition Gucci Dionysus bag was sold as an NFT for $4,115. The sale included exclusive ownership of the digital asset and a physical version of the bag.

12. NFT Collectibles –

Axie Infinity is a blockchain-based game where players can buy, breed, and battle virtual creatures called Axies. In February 2021, rare Axies were sold as NFTs for over $300,000, marking one of the most expensive NFT sale

13. NFT Sports Moments –

NBA Top Shot sold NFT highlights of basketball games for millions of dollars in 2021.

14. NFT Art from Legendary Musicians-

Grimes sold NFT artworks for over $6 million in March 2021.

15. The World's First NFT Horse Race

The virtual horse racing game ZED Run sold NFT horses for over $100,000 in May 2021.

16. NFTs for Access-

The musician Deadmau5 sold NFTs that provided exclusive access to his concerts for over $900,000 in March 2021.

17. The NFT Wine Collection –

The wine company Chateau Brane-Cantenac sold a collection of NFTs featuring its wine labels for over $300,000 in June 2021.

18. NFT Digital Real Estate-

The blockchain-based platform SuperWorld sold virtual real estate as NFTs for over $1 million in February 2021.

.

19. NFTs for Social Media –

The social media platform Rarible sold NFTs that granted exclusive access to its features for over $300,000 in February 2021.

20. The NFT Virtual Reality Game –

 The blockchain-based game The Sandbox sold NFT virtual land for over $2 million in March 2021.

21. NFTs for Sustainable Development –

The digital artist Krista Kim sold NFTs to fund sustainable development projects for over $700,000 in April 2021.

22. The NFT Comic Book –

The comic book company DC sold a Batman-themed NFT artwork for over $1.5 million in June 2021.

23. NFTs for Charity –

The musician Grimes sold NFTs to benefit the Carbon180 non-profit for over $6 million in March 2021

From the case studies above, it is clear to see that the potential and possibilities for serious minded creators are endless. If creation is initiated from a stand point of creating value and quality for an audience that would appreciate your kind of art, Non fungible tokens become an extremely powerful way for creators to monetize their creations.

.

9 A BEGINNER'S GUIDE TO NFT COLLECTING AND INVESTING

NFTs have become a popular investment opportunity in recent years. These digital assets are unique, scarce, and can be sold or traded on blockchain marketplaces. NFTs have become increasingly popular for artists, musicians, and other creators who can monetize their digital works by creating NFTs. In this chapter, we'll provide you with a comprehensive guide to getting started as an NFT collector or investor.

Understanding the NFT Market

Before you start investing in NFTs, it's essential to understand the NFT market. NFTs are a relatively new concept, and the market is still evolving. It's important to do your research and stay informed about the latest developments.

To get started, you can follow news sources, blogs, and social media accounts dedicated to NFTs. You can also join online communities and forums to connect with other NFT enthusiasts and learn more about the market.

Choosing the Right NFTs to Invest In

The key to successful NFT investing is choosing the right assets to invest in. Some of the most popular NFTs include digital art, music, sports collectibles, and gaming assets. When choosing NFTs to invest in, you should consider the following factors:

Rarity and uniqueness: NFTs that are rare or unique are more valuable and can potentially generate higher returns on investment.

Popularity and demand: NFTs that have a strong community following and a history of high sales prices are more likely to appreciate in value over time.

Creator reputation:

The reputation of the creator can impact the value of the NFT. Established creators with a proven track record of success are likely to produce more valuable NFTs.

Evaluating the Potential ROI

It's essential to evaluate the potential return on investment (ROI) before investing in an NFT. To evaluate the ROI, you should consider the following factors:

Historical sales prices: Look at the historical sales prices of similar NFTs to get an idea of how much you might be able to sell your asset for in the future.

Potential for future growth: Consider the potential for future growth and popularity of the asset. For example, if the creator has a history of producing successful NFTs, their future NFTs may also appreciate in value.

Fees and commissions: Be sure to consider the fees and commission rates charged by the platform when evaluating the ROI.

Navigating the NFT Marketplaces

There are several NFT marketplaces available, each with its own unique features and advantages. Some of the most popular marketplaces include OpenSea, Rarible, and Nifty Gateway. When navigating these marketplaces, consider the following factors:

Fees and commissions: Each platform charges fees and commissions for buying and selling NFTs. Be sure to consider these costs when evaluating your ROI.

User experience: The user experience of the platform can impact your ability to find and purchase the NFTs you want.

Platform reputation: Consider the reputation of the platform before making a purchase. Established platforms with a proven track record of success are typically safer investments.

10 AN NFT CASE STUDY FOR THE FUTURE

My fascination with the block-chain was birthed when I watched a video by world re-known speaker and wealth coach, James Altucher, where he brought up powerful arguments about the future of crypto-currency.

I was already aware of the fact that there is very little reason to trust regular currency because unfortunately, it is no longer real money.

It is a gloomy fact that the currencies of the world are doomed to a destiny of devaluation since currency ceased to be real money. The control of governments over fiat where they sometimes dangerously cause inflation by indiscriminate creation of currency is a real problem.

Gold and silver are referred to by Robert Kiyosaki as God's own money. This is because they have two characteristics a true store of value should have, scarcity and real intrinsic value. James Altucher argued that with the growing distrust of human civilizations for their government's economic decisions especially on issues of the economy and money, coupled with man's increasing trust for data driven systems, it was only inevitable for the value and adoption of crypto currency to grow over the years. Notwithstanding the present volatility of crypto currencies, there has been a steady upward climb in value over the years since the advent of Satoshi's Bitcoin innovation till date.

However, I must confess that my fascination has actually been from the sidelines. In 2017, I attended an event hosted at the Sheraton Hotels Abuja on Crypto currency and the blockchain to acquire a little more understanding of the space.

A number of speakers shared valuable information on the potential value of the block chain with the numerous mind boggling possibilities. A particular creator shared how they were creating a fin-tech app that would make international payments amazingly seamless based on the block chain. I really didn't understand all the tech details, but what seemed interesting was that the payments would be made and received by users in regular currency and not necessarily crypto currency but the system would be driven by the blockchain in the back end.

People talked of the possible applications of the block chain smart contracts and possibilities of the block chain helping to improve the security of election monitoring processes, making them fail safe and rigging proof (such possibilities would definitely sound interesting to Nigerians considering a history of very controversial elections).

A great number of speakers came to advertize their newly launched coins which were meant to take the market by storm. It is worthy of note that many of those new coin Ideas were actually scams or possibly well intended projects that possibly did not just make it. However, something notable happened at that event. A company known as Paxful that simply provided a wallet and a supervised peer to peer platform for crypto currency exchange, having a vision for the whole world, but a special focus for the 3rd world and unbanked communities made a presentation on how simple it was for anyone to buy or sell bitcoin or ethereum without a crazy learning curve. This appealed to me. I remember buying about N25, 000 worth of Bitcoin in a paxful account.

I sincerely totally forgot about the account and money for a while. At that time it was money I could afford to lose. A few years later, I remembered my little stash and decided to check the paxful account. The money had grown to about N280,000, This was over 10 times my initial deposit and it happened passively. Now I know it would be possible to, make much more money if I was actively trading my coin investment, but this experience was a strong statement for me. It made me remember James Altucher's arguments again. True, the market is volatile, but over time, values will increase and there will be increased adoption.

The true potential is not just in crypto currency, but what is possible with the block chain. The advent of NFTs which with proper understanding, are a creators haven, is proof of this.

I have a face-book friend, Onas who is an innovative tech furniture creator. His company creates beautiful furniture, but they go ahead to incorporate innovative technology gadgets in the furniture to make them more comfortable and valuable. He made one of their products into a Non Fungible Token that was valued and sold for about $400,000. That example was quite fascinating considering the Naira to Dollar exchange rate at the time. The NFT concept gave his creativity access to a global market that could truly appreciate his great work. This truly had special meaning for me.

If creators can truly creatively package value, Non Fungible Tokens have created a powerful borderless opportunity to share that value with an appreciative audience and get handsomely rewarded.

An NFT opportunity of the future and Three Generations of Super Hero Geeks.

One of the books that have made an extremely powerful impact on me is Robert Kiyosaki's Best Selling book, *Rich Dad, Poor Dad*. It was fascinating to hear him mention on an interview, that Rich Dad Poor Dad was actually intended as an innovative sales brochure to sell the cash flow game that his company created. That revelation actually blew me away.

This book started around my personal research to understand NFTs for a particular reason:

I was an ardent super hero geek as a child. The world of marvel super heroes such as The Avengers, Spiderman, Mighty Thor and their DC counterparts was an arena to let my young fertile imagination run wild, I would also stretch my young imagination to creating my own super hero characters with their own fun origin stories, alter egos and super powers. When most of the comic books started evolving into movies around the time I grew older, got married and started having kids, it was level two of geek paradise for me.

You can imagine how exciting it was when my three kids inherited my "Super Hero Geekism". The origin stories, super powers and plots of these Marvel and DC characters became something fun we could discuss together and explore the possibilities. Questions like "who is a stronger villain? Thanos or Darkseid" became major issues for deep analysis, discussion and debate. I guess for some people, this might seem weird, but I believe a set of people reading this understand exactly what I mean.

My kids especially my two sons Emmanuel and David also soon began to create their own super heroes. Surprisingly, these heroes seemed more realistic, dynamic and interesting than those I tried to create when I was young. Their elder sister Deborah was a great artist, so she would also pitch in helping with the art and stories. Most of the time, they would ask my suggestions considering the character plots and it was fun to pitch in to build this wonderful world of fantasy.

We have created a whole set of characters and stories, the plan is to build a legacy as and possibly more beautiful than the Marvel and DC legacies through a digital and print comic book company with characters and stories that will evolve into movies games and a whole lot of beautiful and valuable intellectual property.

Possibly, when I am a grand-father, their children might join our super hero geek party. Even if they do not, that is still fine, I know there will always be a generation of superhero geeks to have fun, and I know there will be a family where three generations will have the opportunity to bond together over Super hero characters created by a family that had this beautiful bonding experience.

Our plan is to include you on this journey that will span 3 generations or more with the power of NFTs. In the case studies, there is an example of a Batman NFT that was valued as millions of dollars. The gaming industry is also a great opportunity. We also have the advantage of time, just as how wine grows in value as it ages, these NFTs created around the comic book characters will grow in value as the comic book characters and the company of these amazing children and their stories grow with age.

We have decided to include you in the NFT offer creation process so that it becomes our joint project. You also have the advantage of being some of the earliest adopters when the projects launch, imagine having access to own the first ever digital art of King Arctic years before the character is made into a movie? Or owning NFT resell rights to a best seller computer game of the Ultra Squad created years before the comic book and movies became a household name? But as I said, we are creating the possibilities together,

We are creating a community to include you in our creative process and also avail you early access to benefit from this opportunity, of course, I know different people reading this at different times will have opportunity to join us on this journey at different stages, but you are welcome to come behind the scenes into this exciting journey of creation and opportunity.

Click the link or visit www.3genNFT.com to join the family

Also If you are a creator hoping to monetize your creation through NFTs and you would love some help and guidance, feel free to visit www.nfts4creatives.com our resource centre to help you on your creative journey.

ABOUT THE AUTHOR

Dr Asuquo Hogan-Bassey is a Digital Creator, Personal Development Coach and Digital Marketing Consultant. He is founder of the ED Solutions Agency, The Unfair Advantage Secrets Program and Evolve U Personal Protection Dog Evolution Program. He is also founder of Nfts for Creatives, a platform to help creators monetize their creations as non-fungible tokens.

As a prolific creator and entrepreneur himself, he is on a mission to help entrepreneurs scale their businesses with the power of the internet and an unstoppable mindset. He holds a degree in Veterinary Medicine from the University of Ibadan and is married to his lovely wife Prisca Hogan-Bassey with three amazing children, Deborah, Emmanuel and David.

www.ingramcontent.com/pod-product-compliance
Lightning Source LLC
Chambersburg PA
CBHW082228290526
45794CB00009B/3720